TRAUMA DEFAULT

Get a Clear Vision of Your Future by Breaking the Trauma Cycle of Your Past

Christy Rutherford

Copyright © 2020 by: Christy Rutherford

All Rights Reserved. This book or any portion thereof may not be reproduced or used in any manner whatsoever including photocopy, email for fax, except for by the purchaser for personal use, without the express written permission of the publisher except for the use of brief quotations in a book review.

Disclaimer: The information in this book is based on facts, research, and personal experiences. This information is not intended to diagnose, prevent, treat or cure any disease. Never dismiss any advice your health physician gives. The author shall in no event be held liable for any loss or other damages including but not limited to special, incidental, consequential or any other damages.

ISBN-13: 978-1-7359460-0-9

First Edition for Print October 2020

Special thanks to Taurea Avant and the Show Your Success team for bringing this book to life.

THANK YOU

To God, the Universe, Source, Infinite Intelligence, or whatever the world chooses to call the Supreme Being. With you, all things are possible

My family for their endless support and love

My ancestors, for imparting the knowledge of this book and inspiring me to write it

My mentors, and the countless iconic leaders that have mentored me through their books and videos.

CONCEPTS

About the Author 1
Foreword 3
What Is Trauma Default? 5
Trauma Default Stories 9
Channel Pain Into Fuel 13
Awaken to Your Infinite Greatness 17
You Are Two Victims 21
The Kingdom of God Is Within You 23
Soul and Physical Agreement - Authentic Empowerment ... 25
Come as You Are 29
It Is Your Birthright to Be Rich 31
Why People Lose Sudden Wealth 33
The Wealthy Reinforce This in Their Children 35
Believe With the Mind of a Child 37
Do You Want to Be Rich? 39
No One Can Steal Your Shine 41
Hurting People Hurt People 43
Your Body Is Your Temple 45
Whose Words Do You Believe 47
Answer the Call to Be Greater 49
The Catalyst for Awakening 51
The God You Versus the Physical You 53
Broken Past or New Future 55
Conquer the Voice in Your Head 57
Be Ye Transformed by the Renewing of Your Mind 61
What Is TRUTH? 65

Take Responsibility for Where You Are Right Now 67

You've Been Misdiagnosed. Bitterness Is Your Medical Condition 69

Depression Is Destiny Suppression 73

Toxic Relationships 75

Self-Discovery Is a Lonely Journey 77

Perpetual Cycle of Growth and Awakening 79

Break the Cycle and Move to the Next Level 83

Let the Dead Bury the Dead 85

Your Freedom Will Convict the Bondage of Others 87

Forgiveness Is a Lonely Road 91

Child-Like Faith 95

Children Are Unapologetic 97

Five Years of Growth 99

Criticism Destroys Your Seed of Greatness 101

It's Pruning Season for Friends 103

Friendships Created and Nourished in Pain 105

Be Responsible for the Energy You Put In the World 107

Avoid Energy Vampires 109

Dare to Stand Alone 111

Get a New Circle 113

The Imposter Syndrome 115

High Striker 117

People See Who You See 119

Trauma Default Battles at Work 121

Being Devalued at Work 123

When Thou Art Converted, Strengthen Thy Brethren. 125

Life Is Short and Unpredictable 127

ABOUT THE AUTHOR

A globally recognized leader, Christy Rutherford is a trusted coach and mentor to executive leaders and assists them with being promoted through office politics and self-care.

A keynote speaker, she engages her audiences with high energy and wit. Christy published five #1 best-selling books on Amazon in eight months.

A Harvard Business School Alumna, Christy is also a certified Executive Leadership Coach from Georgetown University and has been featured in Forbes three times.

Christy is the 13th African American woman to achieve the rank of Commander (Lieutenant Colonel equivalent) in the U.S. Coast Guard's 225+ year history, where her demographic was (point) .1%.

She responded to the needs of the citizens in New Orleans two days after Hurricane Katrina and had a 3-year Congressional Fellowship with Congressman Elijah Cummings at the House of Representatives.

Christy's academic portfolio also includes an MBA and a pastry chef diploma. Among her many professional accomplishments, her national recognition includes Harvard Business School's 2018 Launching New Ventures Pitch Contest Grand Master Champion, Cambridge Who's Who

Amongst Executives and Professionals, and the Edward R. Williams Award for Excellence In Diversity.

ChristyRutherford.com

Free Case Study: ChangeNowWithChristy.com

FOREWORD

We are on the cusp of extraordinary change in 2020, but a lot of people only see the challenges. The world is always evolving in extraordinary change, and the people who can shift their mindset to see the opportunity in the shifting tide will always fare better.

This has been an impactful year for sure, and we have lost many great leaders like Kobe Bryant, Chadwick Boseman, and Congressman John Lewis, to name a few. In these unprecedented times of a worldwide pandemic, economic crisis, racial injustice, and job crisis, you can descend into the chaos of the world, or you can rise into the leader you are meant to be.

Please remember most great leaders were created during challenging times – Dr. Martin Luther King during the civil rights movement, Madame CJ Walker during Jim Crow, and Kwame Nkrumah during Ghana's struggle for independence. What made these people and millions of others evolve into their highest self was turning a blind eye to challenges and focusing their vision on opportunities.

In *Trauma Default*, Christy Rutherford shares insight on how to break generational cycles that have been in your family for generations. She inspires you to look within and discover your untapped potential to be greater.

Christy is someone whom I highly admire and respect. We spoke at the same conference a few years ago, and I know my biggest value of the conference was meeting her. She is an incredible speaker, a phenomenal trainer, and a bestselling author, but most importantly, she is a good person. She's just good, and I'm proud to call her a mentee and a friend.

I cannot wait to see how this book will impact you and your rise into abundance and opportunity. Use these days of unprecedented change to create disruption in yourself. Become aware of who you are meant to be in this world.

This book will awaken your greater self and give you the blueprint to break the generational curses in your family forever.

Paul Carrick Brunson
Serial Entrepreneur, Television Host
USA Today Columnist

WHAT IS TRAUMA DEFAULT?

After talking to hundreds of highly successful people working in executive leadership positions, I noticed a pattern. (1) Some of them had no idea how great they were. (2) They thought success would feel different. (3) They felt stuck and like they were going in circles. (4) Regardless of their position, salary, and how many degrees they had, they did not feel successful.

They were successful but unfulfilled and could not articulate how they secretly felt something was missing, regardless of their success and material possessions.

They felt guilty for not being happy with having it all; shame for not being able to confess to their family and friends that they were unhappy. As time passed and the number of conversations increased, it all led back to their childhood.

In my career as a former maritime emergency responder, we searched for the root cause of accidents. As a pollution responder, while certain people were worried about the ducks that had oil on them and others were concerned with the oil washing up on beaches, our first concern was to figure out the oil source so we could stop it.

As an incident manager (similar to 911 for accidents on the water), if a ship hit a bridge or caught on fire, I had to take in 100 details from various sources to paint a macro-level picture of who, what, when, and how. Then, I had to whittle down the details and create a three-minute brief for my leaders to recommend how we should proceed forward.

When it came to major accidents, during the investigation, we would discover there were systematic patterns of mistakes. When they were added to a series of small events, something catastrophic would happen. This is true in most major disasters.

With that, I am wired to listen to people, get a macro-level vision for their life, look for the patterns, find the source, and then tell a short story of what happened with recommendations to fix it.

Working with clients, I have noticed the same patterns of major disasters show up in human behavior. Having the opportunity to dig deeper into people's psyche and put together these seemingly small events, they are usually rooted in one or two events.

When people face challenges in relationships or at work and cannot seem to get ahead, they are solving the wrong problem. The 15 or so problems they have in their adult life are rooted in one to two events from their childhood. The root cause – their Trauma Default.

Trauma default is the setting that people go to when they are under pressure, stressed out, or have to take risks. The voice in their head gets louder and reminds them of the times they have failed. They hear a recording of someone saying, "You're going to fail."

"You'll never make it."

"Who do you think you are?" or any other self-defeating phrase that talks them out of playing bigger.

Visual images flash into their head of a traumatic experience; being beaten as a child, sexually abused, impoverished, a refugee, hungry, or homeless. It doesn't have to be abuse or severe physical trauma. It can also be one of seeing their father walkout, their mom depressed or feeling rejected by family or like an outsider as a child and playing alone.

Maybe they were the oldest child of six that felt responsible for the rest of the children and felt like they did not have a proper childhood. It can also be the sixth child that was told they were the surprise baby who adopted a feeling of not being wanted.

The "trauma" is based on the perspective of the child. It is true in their mind and is their **perception** of what happened, whether or not it happened that way. Children believe they are invincible, and when an event occurs that breaks them of that belief, that is what they carry with them for years to come.

People who carry the pain of their childhood are not living in the present moment. They are living through the lens of their painful past. They are so busy focusing on who they don't want to be that they give no thought to who they want to be. They can't adequately feel all they've accomplished because they're still feeling the wounds of their past. The struggle between **who the world sees** and **who the voice in their head condemns** becomes more challenging as people get older, and the pressures of life increase.

A rich person can feel like a pauper if their trauma default is connected to being poor in their childhood. A woman who feels rejected by her father will carry that rejection into her relationships and, ultimately, her marriage. Then, the same pattern will occur as she complains that her spouse rejected her. But the story will be identical to the story of the rejection from her father.

TRAUMA DEFAULT STORIES

One client had a father that was abusive to her mom. When they got divorced, she wanted to live with her father, and he said no. Although she saw him regularly, she lived the next 30 years feeling rejected by her father, not realizing that he likely spared her the same abuse he inflicted on her mom. When she got a clear understanding of that from her rational adult mind, her self-confidence skyrocketed, and she started making powerful moves with fearlessness.

I had an extraordinarily successful businessman that lacked confidence regardless of how many degrees and titles he obtained. He always sought feedback and approval from his peers and leaders and wanted them to pat him on the back after each sales brief. They grew weary of his thirst for support.

He grew up in a middle-class family in Somalia, and when the country went to war, they ended up becoming refugees for two years. He was 10, but the trauma of that event haunted him well into adulthood.

He sought approval in the faces of people during his sales briefs. If he could not feel their support or see their non-verbal cues, his confidence would tank, and then the meeting would go awry.

I discovered the unconscious script that played in his head. When he felt pressure, he unknowingly thought that if they did not like him, he would get fired and end up living in a tent. The voice in his head was relentless and defeating. When we discovered the incident that kept him trapped in a loop, I asked him, was it true? Would he really go back to living in a tent if he were fired?

After having him assess his financials, even if he got fired, he had enough money saved to sustain his family for over five years. This did not include the money his wife made, so the story was simply untrue. He was set free from that story, and his confidence was strengthened. Owning his new reality and stepping into the greatest version of himself, he garnered greater respect from his colleagues and has since been promoted.

Another client wanted to divorce her husband after 13 years but was guilted by family and friends to remain in the union, regardless of how miserable she was. She met him as a waitress in her early 20's, and he was a busboy. After having sex with him, her guilt was immense because she was a Catholic, and they **had to marry**. The problem with this union?

She was a waitress while working on her profession, but he was a busboy by profession. After 13 years, her ambition drove her to high success levels, but his lack of ambition created significant issues. He was who he was and was not going to change regardless of how much wealth she obtained and the material possessions she provided.

While she felt shame, guilt, and condemnation for wanting a divorce, once she saw the root of the challenges, they were never equally yoked, she was instantly freed and became one of the happiest women I've met.

Lastly, I had a client bullied by her mom and siblings starting in childhood and lasting her entire life. Naturally, she married men that abused her mentally and physically and ended up being bullied at work.

At 60 years old, when she saw how the patterns showed up time and time again in four husbands, countless jobs, and innumerable family disputes, and then in her adult daughter, she decided to break the cycle once and for all.

Let me tell you something. This woman is FREE. Clearly seeing her trauma default and choosing a different action to get a different result, she healed generational pain. Her mom is loving, her siblings are more peaceful, and her daughter's professional career skyrocketed.

At 62 years old, she has been promoted, given raises, bonuses, stock options, and achieved her dream of living in an RV on a lake. She has checked off 50 percent of her bucket list, and on and on. She's a testament that it's never too late to live the life you desire if you are willing to do the internal work.

In *Seat of the Soul*, Gary Zukav talked about the need for Spiritual Psychology. Many of my clients spent years going in circles with therapists and psychiatrists talking about their experiences. Still, they never sought the root cause of their multitude of issues rooted in their trauma default. They were seeking a physical solution for a spiritual problem.

Once we discover and break the trauma default cycle, many of my clients are promoted and receive 30-40 percent raises within three months. Several have been promoted over their boss's boss, one in less than three months.

What happened? Their perspective of themselves changed, and they freed themselves from a vicious cycle of self-limiting beliefs. It changed the foundational belief of themselves and their experiences, and they realized that the story they told themselves their entire lives is no longer valid. Then, they simply OWNED the position and income that has been awaiting the realization of their greatness. Everyone else may have seen it in them, but it was not until they got a clear view of themselves that their results changed.

With a new perspective, their default setting changed from one of a limited vision to see the image of their God selves. They went out and immediately conquered more significant goals because they learned that their biggest obstacles were rooted from within. Woooooooooo. So fun!

What is on the other side of your trauma default?

CHANNEL PAIN INTO FUEL

Using a space shuttle as an analogy, when it is getting ready to take off; it uses the rocket boosters and an immense amount of fuel in the takeoff. The rocket boosters spit out fire and smoke and press to get the shuttle off the ground.

The same pattern occurs for a successful person. Successful people have learned how to channel their pain into fuel to get themselves off the ground. However, their siblings may not rise to the same levels of success. If there are three siblings with a similar experience, one will channel their pain into high success, and the other two will use the same conditions to blame their parents or others for why they did not get off the ground.

Countless successful people have committed suicide or who self-medicate with drugs and alcohol because they never healed their past pain. They never forgave the story of the exact same thing that gave them the fuel to get off the ground. Is that you?

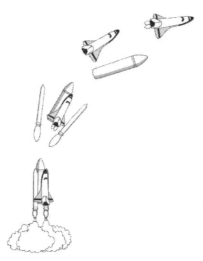

Now think about what happens when the space shuttle gets off the ground. It drops the rocket boosters and, shortly after that, the external tank, right before it goes into space. It doesn't need the extra weight and needs to lighten its load to ascend to the next level. It drops the very same thing it needed to get off the ground.

I'm not sure if this is correct or not but follow me along this line of thinking. If the space shuttle doesn't drop the rocket boosters and fuel tank, will that lead to its demise? Would it be too heavy to ascend and then crash in the ocean?

Let's put it this way. When it comes to your trauma default and the challenges you experienced in childhood, if you don't let go of the same thing you used to get you off the ground, will it lead to your demise? Or will you become stagnant and not able to ascend to the next level?

As you go through this book, I hope you will understand that you needed all of it. Without the painful experiences, you would not have the fuel to lift you off the ground to rise out of the hell you experienced. You knew there was a better life available to you, and you did what it took to achieve it.

Now that you've achieved success, holding onto the past and not forgiving them and yourself will keep you stuck where you are or lead to your demise. Bless your past because it made you who you are today. You needed it. Let it go because YOU MADE it.

Replace the pain that was used as fuel with passion—a passion for being greater and for serving on a greater scale and inspiring others with your story. Inspire them with your healing and forgiveness, and then use your prosperity to be of greater impact to your family and community.

That's where your real prosperity is. Will you pick up the mantle? Finish this book and discover what's waiting for you. Then, find out who is waiting for you to do the work you were called to do.

Successful people have learned how to channel their pain into fuel to get themselves off the ground.

AWAKEN TO YOUR INFINITE GREATNESS

Matthew 13:31-32 –*The Kingdom of Heaven is like a mustard seed, which a man took and planted in his field. Though it is the smallest of all seeds, yet when it grows, it is the largest of garden plants and becomes a tree, so that the birds come and perch in its branches.*

You were born with a seed of greatness and a problem that you are meant to solve for your generation – your purpose. You came here with it inside of you. As a child, it was likely on display, but as you adjusted who you were to fit in, coupled with choosing untrained parents who are suffering from their own trauma, the seed was buried deep into your soul.

Your purpose is the size of a mustard seed, and it is hidden in the darkness of your trauma default. At the point of awakening, you must go back into your darkest place to learn the lesson and retrieve it—your dark place. The chapter of your story you rarely reveal. The chest of secrets you buried in the abyss.

Enter that dark place because that's where your true freedom lives. All precious gems are mined in the darkness. The darkness also holds rats, spiders, and other scary creatures but mines house diamonds, gold, rubies, and emeralds.

Your purpose is the size of a mustard seed, and it is waiting for you. Your physical body is the field that will nurture the seed into fruition, or through neglect, you will destroy it. Create a growth environment and become good ground so you may nurture your seed into full bloom. Invest in your soil and nurture your inner Being to give the seed what it needs to take root and grow.

Mustard seeds grow into large trees, and birds come to perch on its branches. Birds are the people you are meant to touch and heal when you give yourself permission to become the greatest version of yourself.

Dr. Myles Munroe said something like, "A tree doesn't eat its own fruit. A tree feeds its fruit to others, and when they're nurtured and cared for by its fruit, they will bring a portion of their storehouse back to you. That is how you create prosperity."

Your soul is an infinite storehouse of wealth, ideas, and beliefs. It is lying dormant and waiting for your sleeping physical body to awaken and realize your power and possibilities of life. But the first thing that needs to happen is you need to become aware of the cycle that you are trapped in – your trauma default. The cycle that shows up again and again in your life. One that is caused by an event or a cycle of events that creates the pattern for where you are today.

Your trauma default has you trapped in a cycle of unforgiveness, resentment, guilt, shame, and pain of events that are long gone but never forgotten. Those that stay constant and top of mind which are lived daily in an old memory and a new day. How can you ever expect to live a great future if you are always trapped in the thinking of your past?

After reading this book, you can no longer shift the responsibility of your healing to others. You and only you are responsible for this work. Even with this information, most people will not do it. Will you?

The reason why many are called but few are chosen to do this work is because it is easier to blame others than to take 100% responsibility for where you are. Blaming others is sweeter and more refreshing because it is easy. But is it? Being trapped in a cycle for the past 20 - 40 years is not easy, but since you aren't taking full responsibility for it, you may feel that you don't have a choice. I am here to tell you that you do.

It is not easy to look at yourself in the mirror and despise the person looking back at you. Pick up the mantle and decide to take action so you can break the cycle once and for all.

If you do not do it for yourself because you think it's too selfish, do it for your family's unborn children. Do it for the people you are meant to serve with the fragrance of your healing. Make that the sweet perfume of your life and not the stench of an old story that has grown stale and dreary in the dark cave of your past. Pull that story out of the darkness and bring it to Light.

When you become aware of who you are and whom you are meant to serve, you will put together the parts of your broken past and realize that you would not be who you are today without it.

You needed it. You needed all of it. Your spirit wanted to experience it in this physical form so it could learn the lesson. Now, you, physical being, must heal it so that you can heal others. But do not be too hasty to announce your healing. Many people got surface healing and rushed the process. They pretended to be healed for the sake of being seen or famous. Then, they paid a great price as the weight of glory is heavy, but grace is light.

To bear the weight of who you are, who you will be, and the multitude of people who need you, you must be 100% healed, whole, and healthy.

Join Christy's Newsletter and get more insight on Trauma Default

www.bit.ly/traumadefaultinfo

YOU ARE TWO VICTIMS

Living from the place of trauma default makes you unaware that you are two victims - the sufferer and the creator of the suffering. Victimized by your own victimhood.

But you are also your Redeemer and your remedy. Your spiritual problems that have manifested into your physical life and conditions have caused you to self-medicate. Healing from within will free you from what ails you most. Be your physical remedy instead of medication. Become your spiritual Redeemer.

It is your sole responsibility to awaken to this fact and do the work to save yourself. No one in the physical realm can save you from suffering from within. Suffering from a seemingly insignificant event that has been long forgotten about and unhealed, which has shaped your very existence. An event that has shaped your suffering soul's pattern and has put your physical mind and body in bondage.

Your inner Being lies dormant and awaits this realization and desires to awaken. When you have risen to the point of understanding, your inner Being creates discomfort in your physical body because it is ready to heal from that cycle. You will feel something stirring around in you and think you're going mad, but it's the soul stirring to be awakened and wants to emerge and heal so you can solve the problem that you were sent here to solve.

Get busy doing this work to heal your past and then use that healing to go and heal others.

THE KINGDOM OF GOD IS WITHIN YOU

Matthew 6:33 – *Seek ye first the Kingdom and all these things will be added onto you.*

The Kingdom is within you, but many people seek *things* before seeking the Kingdom. If your inner Being was a kingdom, does it look like a Royal palace or a junkyard? Palaces are filled with gold and artifacts and are well maintained by a multitude of people. Palaces have pristine white marble, gold columns, and large halls for the inhabitants.

An abandoned palace is dirty and overrun with weeds. Trees grow through the foundation, and dirt covers the once-great halls. It's likely littered with trash and unwanted things of the people who abandoned it. It will fall into ruin without constant maintenance and care. Have you fallen into ruin by seeking things and not maintaining your palace?

Seeking material possessions does not add adornment to the Kingdom within. It only polishes your outer appearance while your inner Being descends into ruin. People spend large amounts of money on houses, cars, purses, and clothes so they can feel loved, successful, and celebrated.

They get plastic surgery and warp their natural features so they can feel better about themselves. They never actually feel better, and have so much plastic surgery that they become unrecognizable. Even then, they don't feel whole because they only changed their external appearance.

SOUL AND PHYSICAL AGREEMENT - AUTHENTIC EMPOWERMENT

"When the personality comes fully to serve the energy of its soul, that is authentic empowerment." – Gary Zukav

---

The spirit is formless and lives a multitude of lifetimes. It wants to experience everything that life has to offer; the good and the bad. Your spirit chose your physical body with its distinct personality in an effort to have an experience that it hasn't had before.

The spirit carries the energy and unhealed trauma from past lifetimes and arrives in a physical form born to a family with unhealed trauma that can be inherited genetically—scientists call it epigenetics.

It will take multiple lifetimes to heal, so we are never really done—just evolving. Healing is a layered approach. As you heal one layer, you reveal the next. There are different layers between the physical and spiritual realms that need to be healed.

(1) Those we intended to heal when we arrived as spirit.

(2) The generational wounds of our ancestors, and

(3) The new wounds incurred in this lifetime.

If you choose to come into alignment with this work, a vast new world of opportunity is available to you. However, once you become self-aware of the trauma default cycle, you are trapped in and all the elements that have created it, you can drown in the magnitude of challenges that need to be healed.

If you answer the call and choose to do the work, you will be exposed to the unhealed parts of yourself that need to be healed. The process will seem unfathomable as each layer of what needs to be healed is revealed. The weight can be crushing.

To most unconscious people who are not seeking healing through *understanding*, this is where they stop and revert to their old ways because the mountain and level of problems are too high.

Matthew 22:14 – Many are called, but few are chosen

The few chosen are crazy enough and conscious enough to do the work to get to the other side of themselves. A new realm of life is revealed to them—one of infinite choice, freedom, and grace

Grace for self is the most important and then grace for others because you cannot give what you do not have. It is a selfish journey to get healed and whole, and many won't understand it. It is an absolute selfless act so that you will be able to serve in a greater capacity in your God form, using your God capacity. Many are called, but the chosen are few.

Are you willing to be isolated, ostracized, and alone to do the self-work to heal so that you may be a demonstration of God's word to those that you are called to serve?

You are not called to talk to the multitude, only the lost sheep that will know your voice when they hear you. Will you do the work to purify your spirit so that God may re-enter and use you as a physical expression of Himself to heal others?

It is a selfish journey to get healed and whole, and many won't understand it.

COME AS YOU ARE

You do not have to be perfect when you start this work. In fact, the more broken you are and the more challenges you have experienced, the better because your healing will speak louder than any words you can utter from your mouth. You do not have to get ready or perform certain rituals to prepare yourself. You just have to be open and willing to heal yourself so that you may be used to heal others.

You are God's most remarkable work. Healing will allow you to be used by the Creator for greater work to serve those that you are meant to serve. That's where your real prosperity lies, not only in money but in the fulfillment of your life's purpose and passion. Genuinely helping those you are meant to serve and being where you are celebrated for your gifts while distancing yourself from places where you are tolerated.

When you start the healing journey to be a catalyst for change, you will stop shrinking your energy and your potential to fit into small places and with small-minded people, you were never meant to fit in with—this includes family members too.

A note to consider... You cannot save those who are kin to you - sameness. Most of them will never see you in your glory, and it is not your responsibility to save them. Jesus was not a prophet in His own land. Leave that up to God and know that the service will be rendered to your family by another person who will impact them through the work you do. By the Law of Karma, what you sow will come to them.

When you heal a part of who you are, you break that cycle and bond of dysfunction that has plagued your family for generations. Your work heals the energy to all children born in your family forever. They will start at a higher level to propel your family to even higher heights and create a lineage of even greater Kings and Queens.

IT IS YOUR BIRTHRIGHT TO BE RICH

Most poverty starts in the mind long before it materializes in your physical and outer condition. You believed the lie that you were told in your childhood because you were born a woman, handicapped, a person of color, or whatever you choose to adopt as an excuse for your limitations.

There are plenty of people of color who have broken through the bonds of limited thinking and claimed their birthright. People who were born without arms and legs have expressed themselves through art and music. Helen Keller lost her sight and hearing when she was 19 months old, but eventually became one of the iconic thought leaders of all time.

Choosing to tap into the greatness within, despite the limitations of the physical body, has propelled more people forward than any lottery winning. Tap into the gold mine that's within you, and you will no longer seek to satiate your innate desire to have more with get rich quick schemes, winning the lottery, or suing companies for whatever ridiculous condition. It is your birthright to be rich, but you thought that someone else should give it to you.

Matthew 18:19 - *Again, truly I tell you that if two of you on earth agree about anything they ask for, it will be done for them by my Father in heaven.*

Your inner Being knows this as a fact, but your physical form has to agree with your inner Being. The two people on earth that need to agree are your inner Being and your physical form.

You were born rich, so you do not have to seek it from others. It is within you.

Your buried treasure.

Your untapped potential.

Your unique gift to bring to the world.

Have you become too busy or distracted to seek what is already within you? You don't have to rediscover yourself. You need to *remember* yourself and the greatness that you were born with despite your physical conditions. The supply is not limited. Your thinking is.

WHY PEOPLE LOSE SUDDEN WEALTH

Your desire to be rich without reconnecting with your God Being is like a peasant wearing all the adornments of royalty but never actually feeling connected with the new outer conditions of wealth.

It is real wealth, but the peasant's physical body doesn't remember its inherent right for wealth by spiritual form. It will eventually forfeit all that they have obtained simply because they don't remember that they were really meant to be rich.

They will feel guilty or condemn themselves. They will feel like a fraud or impostor because of the unawakened state or realization that it is their right to be rich. A birthright bestowed upon those who quickly remember that they are spiritual Beings having a physical experience.

Could this be why so many people who get sudden wealth are bankrupt within three to five years? Lottery winners, professional sports players, singers, and entertainers who obtain sudden wealth tend to lose it quickly.

Many professional athletes and singers started working on their craft when they were five or six years old. They can feel within them that they are meant to be great and prosperous. They seek wealth and fame and work arduously to obtain it. When it finally happens as adults, they celebrate all the hard work externally, but many didn't do the inner work. Their inner Beings get caught up in the plight of their physical form and the external challenges and struggles they had to endure until they finally made it.

So, subconsciously and unconsciously, they purge themselves of their money. They feel undeserving of receiving the money, cars, and houses, regardless of how hard they worked for it. They rose out of the ashes of poverty and felt guilty because they made it, and others did not.

THE WEALTHY REINFORCE THIS IN THEIR CHILDREN

Wealthy people teach their children it is their right to be rich. They know it as a fact and prepare their children for all the things that they need to do to receive the wealth that is inherently theirs. People may label this as being "entitled," but it is true for you too.

It is hard for people born into poverty to adopt this belief because their surroundings and environment don't support it. The words go unuttered and unspoken, but that does not mean the words do not exist. They have been around for centuries in the ether. The words of your inherent right to be rich have been around since the beginning of hieroglyphics and other ancient writings that talked about the souls and reconnecting with self.

One of the challenges that African Americans have is that we forgot where we came from. It was beaten out of our ancestors, and their memory slates were wiped clean of the rituals to tap into our God selves from within and tap into our spiritual place for guidance and direction in our lives.

All of that was lost while they suffered in the dungeons of slave ships. It was beaten out of them until they forgot or stopped talking about being true Kings and Queens and Gods from within. Their language was taken away, and they were not allowed to read or write.

While they could not pass this information down generationally, the right to be rich was never forfeited. That has not been lost upon us, simply forgotten. Awaken to your true self and nature from within. It is not as much a battle as it is a *remembering*.

Not by the works of man but by the works of your God within. Believe it and get into alignment with who you are meant to be and the great acts you were born to demonstrate in this lifetime. It is never too early, and it is never too late. It's merely the capacity to step into who you are already capable of being.

BELIEVE WITH THE MIND OF A CHILD

Kids today, Mikaila Ulmer – Bees Lemonade, CoryNieve – Cory's cookies, and Ryan Kaji – YouTube's Ryan ToysReview, are demonstrating and living in the desire and the blessings that they were born with.

Kids are creative. If they have an environment to flourish in with their big dreams and a supportive family, then the inner wealth they were born with spiritually can be materialized in their physical experience much easier.

The challenge is when kids are born into conditions of limited-thinking parents and friends of parents who are ignorant of the fact that we were all born rich. The simple idea to make cookies, lemonade, or review toys is their idea to bring to fruition. They are meant to impact the world, and they know it. Many children lose their ability to believe in themselves when they adopt their parents' limited thinking and beliefs.

There's no better time than now to rise out of poverty through hard work and determination. Billionaires like Oprah, Tyler Perry, Howard Shultz, and J.K. Rowling were born into poverty and conquered the limited and traumatic conditions of their childhoods. The inherent desire to be great, and prosperous has driven many people to achieve far more than they could have achieved with their minds alone.

It has also created many crooks and Ponzi schemes. It drives the desire for people to rob, kill, and destroy others for their resources. For the pilgrims to pillage the Indians. For whites to steal slaves from a land and then ravage its continent for centuries.

It's the desire to be rich that wants to express itself through physical form. But how the riches are obtained determines whether or not a person is truly satisfied spiritually when they receive them.

Was it the plan of their God form that created the wealth, or was it happenstance and obtained quickly? Could this be an underlying reason why a wealthy person can commit suicide despite their vast wealth? Because it was the plan of their physical form, but not their God form? The money did not satiate the desire of their unawakened soul.

Join Christy's Newsletter and get inspired

www.bit.ly/traumadefaultinfo

DO YOU WANT TO BE RICH?

You were born with the capacity to be wealthy. But with the rise of social media, video games, and YouTube, many people have become too distracted to obtain it. They entertain get rich quick schemes or yearn to be like the people who spend their time looking rich in appearance but poor in spirit.

Unhealed, unhealthy, and broken people who glamorize their actual or borrowed material possessions have hypnotized you into believing that obtaining riches is the key to happiness. But real wealth is a by-product of reconnecting with who you were born to be and expressing your God form through this physical body and serving the people you are meant to serve and touch the people you are meant to touch.

Many people have expressed their gifts and become wealthy through social causes. Tom's Shoes became wealthy by making shoes and giving away a pair when someone bought a pair.

Real wealth is a by-product of service. The more people you serve, the more money you make. Some people only want to serve themselves and cannot fathom why they can't get ahead or remain on the bottom. It's because of their desire to be rich is to show others that they are rich. They do not even want to be rich for themselves as much as they want to be rich for others.

To demonstrate their lack of value for themselves, they spend their money to impress others, but they are not even impressed with themselves. They do not engage in movements to create social change. Their desire for change is solely about being better *than* others rather than being better *for* others. They are never greater than others because they are not great for themselves.

NO ONE CAN STEAL YOUR SHINE

A spiritual Being enlightened in its true form knows that it is unique and does not seek to outshine others. It does not have to because it has plenty of Light to illuminate the cosmos. Light seeks Light and does not get inundated by the Light of others or try to diminish their shine.

Light attracts Light, so many Light Beings seek each other in the quest for more significance and will push and propel each other, never uttering a word of deceit or giving up their quest to reclaim their Queendom or Kingdom from within.

We need people who are on a spiritual journey to support the awakened process. It will be futile to allow a limited-thinking person to thwart the mission that comes from within. It is an intentional mission that you must seek for yourself, but you don't have to be by yourself.

Do not be afraid if you don't have anyone to support you. Support yourself. Rise from within. Reclaim your greatness. It is within you, and no one can reach in and pull it out for you. No one can claim it for you.

Do not sink into despair or allow the internal battle for self to be mislabeled or diagnosed as a medical condition. Do not self-medicate your soul to sleep. Do not doom yourself with distractions. Focus and align yourself to claim your heritage and birthright as a spirit, regardless of your physical form.

You chose your limitations as a spiritual Being before you entered this physical realm. You selected them to overcome them, not sink into them, and adopt them as reasons you are not where you want to be. A newer and better reality is available to you. It always has been. Remember *who* you are is not *where* you are.

HURTING PEOPLE HURT PEOPLE

The people at your job or your spouse is not the root cause of your vexation. Your unhealed trauma is. They are merely magnifying the pain point that you haven't addressed. In many ways, it is the unhealed parts of their inner Being that create pain for you. It's true when they say, "Hurting people hurt people."

How long are you going to allow hurting people to hurt you? They will criticize the way that you look because they have a distorted view of themselves. They criticize the way you talk because they don't have anything meaningful to say. Your peace convicts their chaos. Your confidence convicts their insecurity. Your external beauty convicts the ugliness of their soul.

There is no shortage of hurting people in the world, and if you are waiting for others to get whole before you can have peace, then you will wait your whole life.

Taking it one layer deeper, the number of haters you have is truly a reflection of how you feel about yourself. The more haters you have, the more you hate yourself. An African proverb says, "When there is no enemy within, the enemy outside can do you no harm."

When you heal and become whole, you will be less triggered by others. You will have compassion for them because you know they are suffering, and in their suffering, they are attempting to make you suffer. You can choose whether you allow them to impose their pain on you or offer them grace, forgive them, and let them go about their way.

YOUR BODY IS YOUR TEMPLE

Do you treat your car better than your body? Do you clean your house but do not clean your heart? Do you throw away unnecessary things to get rid of clutter, but you don't declutter your mind and soul by forgiving others? It's time to let go of

(1) The transgressions of the past.

(2) The transgressions of others, and

(3) Your transgressions – the most important.

Too often, people shrink to make others like them to the point that they feel they are nothing, useless, or a nobody. But anyone who still has breath in their body can be used for a higher purpose if they choose to get healed and do the work.

It is a process that's tedious as you have to peel back the layer of the unhealed parts of yourself to review each level, and then the next level, and then another level until you get to what the real core issue is. That's a slow way.

The fastest way is to become aware of the story that you are telling yourself daily. When you want to do something big or step out and be greater, is your inner voice supportive or demeaning? Is this story aligned with who God says you are, or is it speaking to the limitations and small thinking of your physical form?

The more important question to ask is, why do you believe the demeaning voice more than the words that have been spoken to you from your inner Being since birth? You are a King or Queen. You are wealthy beyond measure and free.

WHOSE WORDS DO YOU BELIEVE

Do you believe that you are downtrodden and unforgiven? Have you adopted the belief of what someone else said about you and forgotten about what the Creator said about you? Made perfect in His image. Did you forget the Big You that came into this physical form to solve a big problem - your spiritual self?

You adopted the belief of someone with a limited vision of themselves. Therefore, they transferred their limited belief onto you, and you believed them because you forgot yourself. No one outside of you can tell you who you are. You need to *remember* who you are and why you are here and not believe the small words of an unhealed and unawakened Being.

Someone who has awakened to their greatness knows that we are all meant to be great and will not speak ill will of you or others because we know the truth. We know that we are not in competition with anyone, and we are all uniquely created to solve a problem. Together we can get it done faster. So, collaboration is imperative for us to fulfill our mission.

An awakened Being speaking death to your dreams knows that we are speaking death to our dreams and will not do it because we understand that karma is real. We will not criticize, ostracize, minimize, or allow you to live smaller than who you are fully capable of being. It is not in the nature of the healed and awakened to speak ill of you because we know that it will come back to us.

Be aware of the people who pretend to be healed and awakened. They will show you who they are with their actions and words. Have the courage to leave them the first time they say something negative or condescending. When you are looking to be healed and awakened, you have no time to waste when it comes to being around anyone who will speak death into your dreams.

Distance yourself from them at once. However, forgive them, for they know not what they do. They may not be aware that they have a different choice to make and that they can embark on a similar journey. However, be mindful because you cannot convince them or make them join you on this quest. This is a journey that you must be willing to go alone for a season. You will need to learn self-reliance and understand that you are never really alone.

You have the Supreme Being on your side, wanting to work with you to get you into alignment with who you agreed to be as Spirit so He can flow through you to touch who He is meant to touch. By working through you in your gift, you now heal the next person to get them into alignment, so He can flow through them to reach whom they are meant to touch and so on.

ANSWER THE CALL TO BE GREATER

Where would the world be right now if every wounded person heeded the call of their suffering soul that is calling them back home to heal? Calling them from spending useless time on social media, longing to connect with others when they really want to connect with is themselves. One person connected with themselves is greater in power, peace, and prosperity than 20 million followers on Instagram. Bet all your chips on that fact.

When you get reacquainted with who you are meant to be and who you truly are, anxiety, anguish, and depression will be annihilated. Disease cannot exist in the body of a truly enlightened being.

Can your children, spouse, or partner fully connect with you when you are not connected with yourself? Choose to seek peace from within to create harmony in your home. How can you be connected to other people if you aren't connected with yourself? Choose to do this work for yourself so you can be better for others. When you become a better person, you will become a greater mom, dad, daughter, son, brother, sister, cousin, leader, etc. Everything starts with you.

Cleanse yourself from the inside. Change yourself from the inside. Change your circumstances from the inside. Seek inner peace, inner health, and inner healing, and all your outside circumstances will change.

Most people try to change by buying bigger houses. They think buying a new car will make them feel happier or getting married will make them happier. *Seek ye first the Kingdom, and all of these things shall be added unto you.*

Since childhood, you have been sold a lie that if you were married and lived in a big house with a picket fence and a nice car that you will be happy. Now here you are with this big job that's stressing you out, working too much to spend time with your family so you can afford the big house and fancy car, and you're miserable and unhappy. If you are miserable, broke, and single, you will be miserable rich, and married.

Money only magnifies who you are. If you are a giver when you are broke, you will give when you are rich. If you are stingy broke, you will be stingy when you are rich. If you don't pay tithes on $100k, you certainly won't pay them at $10 million.

THE CATALYST FOR AWAKENING

"Many people who are going through the early stages of the awakening process are no longer certain what their outer purpose is. What drives the world no longer drives them. Seeing the madness of our civilization so clearly, they may feel somewhat alienated from the culture around them. Some feel that they inhabit a no-man's-land between two worlds. They are no longer run by the ego, yet the arising awareness has not yet become fully integrated into their lives."

– Eckhart Tolle

When your level of growth exceeds your level of understanding, you will start to question the meaning of life. You will wonder, "Is this it?" "I thought it would feel better than this."

Awakening or the desire to be awakened is when you want to BE different, even if you can't articulate it. It's when you want SOMETHING different, but you don't know what it is. It's your inherent nature to grow and expand, and you may realize that you aren't living in your full potential, and that is no longer acceptable to you. You finally admit that you are miserable with all that you've worked hard for and obtained.

You may feel there is someone calling you, or there's an energy pulling you. You may receive visions or have dreams about a greater life. Even if you don't know what should happen or what your life should feel like, you have a deep knowing that it should be different. When this happens, your inner Being wants to be awakened and take precedence in your life again.

Many are called, but the chosen are few.

Are you listening? Will you answer the call?

There is usually a trauma occurrence that drives the initiative for change. It can be thoughts of suicide, a terminal illness diagnosis, a car accident, or cancer diagnosis. It may be the death of a close friend or relative. It is something that shakes your core and makes you question the true meaning of life. Meditation, stillness, and wanting to heal deep suffering can also create an opening for the spirit to appear.

People either change through inspiration or desperation. Unfortunately, most people change through desperation because change is hard, and it typically takes something traumatic or dramatic to break the script of the story playing in your head.

A new script starts playing, and it is louder than the one that's been playing for years on end. It is a new story that has broken the unconscious psyche and awakened the stirring soul that desires to reemerge. This can happen at any time in your life, so it is never too early or too late. It feels like a desire to surrender your plan for The Plan.

THE GOD YOU VERSUS THE PHYSICAL YOU

Genesis 25:22-23 –Before Rebekah gave birth, she knew she was going to have twins, because she could feel them inside her, fighting each other. She thought, "Why is this happening to me?" Finally, she asked the LORD why her twins were fighting, and he told her, "Your two sons will become two separate nations. (two nations always in conflict)."

The ability to be awakened is always available. However, if that is true, why don't people do it sooner or not at all? Many people self-medicate their awakening or self-awareness out of them because they think they are losing their minds.

Being bi-polar or "of two minds" is the wrong diagnosis for many people. Two souls housed within Rebecca's womb that started fighting before birth may represent the spiritual agreement to enter the physical form with the hopes that the physical body will remember its spiritual origin and eventually reclaim its Godliness.

Many physical beings forget and get so caught up with the plight of their limited form that they just settle for a measly physical life and never activate or remember that with God, all things are possible. Have you forgotten?

Tap into your God form and reconnect with the spiritual side of yourself that wants to take precedence in your life. Get busy solving the problem for humanity you are meant to solve.

The ignorance of (wo)man of its God form allows you to live far below your capacity and desire for greater. If you simply knew and remembered the desires of your spirit, the soul's agreement before you arrived, then you will rise out of the ashes of limited thinking and poverty.

BROKEN PAST OR NEW FUTURE

Which is easier, trying to glue together pieces of a broken vase or using a potter's wheel to create a new one? One involves headaches and frustration to get tiny pieces to fit together, knowing it will never be whole again. The other is new and exciting, even with its imperfections, until the finished work is revealed. What are you choosing for a broken life?

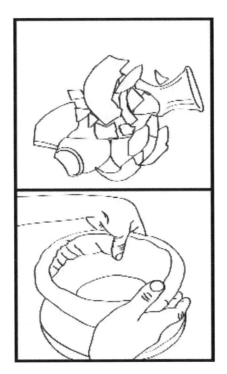

When you get reacquainted with who you are meant to be and who you truly are, anxiety, anguish, and depression will be annihilated.

CONQUER THE VOICE IN YOUR HEAD

"What a liberation to realize that the 'voice in my head' is not who I am. Who am I then? The one who sees that." – Eckhart Tolle

Self-talk is one of the most destructive behaviors and habits you may have. There is an on-going story in your head that reflects your reality or your greatest fears. A lot of emotions can be triggered by self-criticism and the voice in your head.

You know the one I am talking about. The tyrant that talks to you the moment you decide to step outside of your comfort zone and do something new. The voice that shows up and tells you that you do not know what you're doing, you will fail, or you're a loser. It can beat you down and talk you out of doing something before you even begin. Yes, THAT voice.

Being unconscious of the seemingly insignificant trauma event from your past is what shapes your entire reality. That is the perspective you see your life through. It is like walking around with pain colored glasses and attempting to live a whole life.

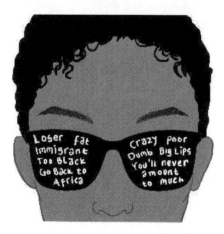

However, when you want to take a risk, step out, and do something bigger, like ask for a promotion or raise, the voice gets louder. It tells you that "You will fail."

"Who do you think you are?"

"You'll never make it."

"You'll look like a fool," and on and on.

I do this exercise with all my clients. I have them meditate, do affirmations, and workout. This is to create self-awareness so they can hear what they have been saying to themselves. One of my clients, a 50-year-old, was astounded at what she heard.

She said, "Christy, I can't believe it! I finally heard myself say, 'You are broke. You are a nobody, and you will never be anybody. You are too old, and you will die broke'."

This script had been playing in her head for a long time. It shaped her decisions to play small and stay in a "secure" government job, even though she was miserable. She knew that she had more potential and could play bigger, but the story that she woke up to and went to bed with kept her trapped in a self-made prison hole. After breaking her trauma default, she left that job and was promoted to the C-suite of an organization she loves.

When your level of growth exceeds your level of understanding, you will start to question the meaning of life.

BE YE TRANSFORMED BY THE RENEWING OF YOUR MIND

"I guarantee you; you are living with the consequences of what you say about yourself." – TD Jakes

---

If you choose to take control of your mind, the voice in your head can be trained. It will take some time, but if you're still alive next year, the time will pass anyway. Why not use it to better your life?

Some people may reject this notion immediately, but is it easier to talk back to the voice in your head and fight for the life you want than it is to let it control you and live in misery?

Let's test it. Please repeat the following statements that pertain to you aloud. If they are things you want, internalize the words. Pause, and observe what the voice says to you.

1. I want to make more money.

2. I want a better job.

3. I want to be happier.

4. I want to be healthier.

5. I want better relationships with a partner and my family and friends.

Was the voice supportive? Did it say something you disagreed with? Would you have liked a better response? Again, it is possible to reprogram your mind, but you will have to become more aware of what you are saying to yourself, so you need to become an observer.

Imagine your mind as a tape recorder. You are the tape recorder and not the tape. If you choose, you can eject the current tape and replace it with another one that tells the story of the life you want.

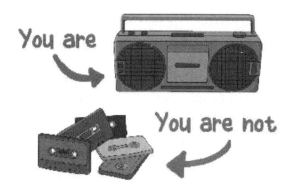

If you are younger than 30 years old, let's use another analogy. You are the music app on your phone. You are not the music that you download. Choose to delete the songs you no longer want and download positive songs that make you feel good about yourself.

In his phenomenal book *Psycho-Cybernetics*, Dr. Matthew Maltz gave five steps for reprogramming the voice. When your inner voice says something negative, do the following (CRAFT):

1. Cancel – say it aloud

2. Replace – with positive data

3. Affirm – the new image you desire

4. Focus – 10 minutes daily

5. Train – yourself for lasting change

During my early years in entrepreneurship that was wrought with failure, the voice in my head got so loud that it became crushing. The more money I lost, and the more I failed, the louder it got. When the voice said, "You're going to fail and run out of money, "I implemented CRAFT and said, "CANCEL!"

Then, to myself, "I can achieve anything. I choose to serve others and deserve success." Then, I imagined celebrating with my business partners on a yacht or the beach in Bora Bora. I also meditated 10-30 minutes daily.

Stating "CANCEL" aloud startled a few people at the grocery store and bookstore, but I'm sure they were dealing with their own voice. If you want to free yourself from yourself, then be unapologetic about your healing.

There's no better time than now to rise out of poverty through hard work and determination.

WHAT IS TRUTH?

Winston Churchill said, "Truth is incontrovertible. Panic may resent it. Ignorance may deride it. Malice may distort it. But there it is." Let's break down and define the keywords.

The truth is incontrovertible - not able to be denied or disputed.

[Panic] Sudden uncontrollable fear or anxiety, often causing wildly unthinking behavior, causes you to react with bitter indignation at having been treated unfairly [may resent it].

[Ignorance] Lack of knowledge or information allows you to express contempt for it [may deride it].

[Malice] the desire to harm someone or ill will [may] give a misleading or false account or impression of [distort it].

But there it is.

Your soul is an infinite storehouse of wealth, ideas, and beliefs.

TAKE RESPONSIBILITY FOR WHERE YOU ARE RIGHT NOW

There are people who spend hours on the phone complaining about their lives to family and friends. For some, it's a ritual and dumping of emotional baggage to relieve the pain of an unfair life. Whether the pain is created by a friend, relationship, boss, or an encounter with a nasty person, the story is real and justified.

When you tell your friends and acquaintances the story of what happened, your victim status is out of the lens of your trauma default. You seek the person who soothes your pain in that part of your experience, and they will support you. They strengthen the story you tell, but there is a deeper wound that you keep to yourself, and it is the cause of all your problems. It shapes your entire reality.

You only tell one side of the story, which is rooted in your trauma default, so you cannot see the story clearly. The saying, "there are three sides to every story," is true.

1. Your side rooted in your trauma default.

2. Their side rooted in their trauma default.

3. The TRUTH, which is actually what happened.

Friends will agree with you and nurture you, but you must acknowledge the trauma default, know why you react the way you do, and heal it to break the cycle truly. You have to make conscious choices and take different actions to break the trauma default to get a new desired result.

Unconscious actions and reacting from the mind of the wounded child will keep you in a perpetual state of suffering. Only when you address the unconscious wound will you be able to truly free yourself from being a slave to your past and live in the fullness of your present. Then you can create the future you desire and deserve.

Can you genuinely perceive the truth of your present life if it is based on your trauma default? Can you genuinely perceive the truth of your present and past relationships if they are seen through the eyes of your trauma default?

Are you able to see your future if you are wrapped up in a warped reality of your present created by and viewed through the lens of your trauma default? Free yourself and step into the fullness of your destiny.

YOU'VE BEEN MISDIAGNOSED. BITTERNESS IS YOUR MEDICAL CONDITION

Bitter indignation. Being bitter is when something has been marinating for a long time. You don't become bitter about something that happened yesterday. Bitter and resentment are long-held upon stories and feelings that have stewed in your body for years.

Bitterness can be felt in your energy when you walk in the room. You wear it on your face. It's a negative, electric feeling that people don't want to be around. Either you are bitter and sad, telling a woe is me story, or you are bitter and angry and will set it off at any moment. Walking around like a ticking time bomb and living in the spirit of offense, waiting to be offended and then justifiably releasing your anger on those who offended you.

Bitter indignation is a dangerous place to be in because you feel justified in your bitterness. You live in a perpetual cycle of misery, and you make everyone around you miserable. You have a terrible quality of life, and you blame everyone else for it, but the real cause of your misery is you.

Unconsciously acting from bitterness creates depression, anxiety, and a whole host of mental disorders that psychiatrists and medical doctors have doomed people with. Giving them a permanent diagnosis for a spiritual problem.

When you relive a trauma repeatedly, your body emits the same frequencies and chemicals you experienced during the trauma. Just like when you are sleeping, your subconscious mind is active while your conscious mind is sleeping. Your tape is playing on full blast, and your body cannot tell the difference between the truth and a dream.

You may dream that a dog is chasing you or a person is attacking you. Your heart rate increases, and you may start sweating. You breathe hard as you try to escape the dangerous event. When you relive the trauma in your dreams (subconsciously) and then awaken to tell the story, you say it felt so real.

The same happens when you complain about the events of your past or what someone did to you. You are now consciously telling the story, and your body relives the moment and releases the same chemicals. If you were scared in the past event, you could start shaking when you tell the story. If you were angry, you would furrow your brow, and your chest will tighten as you relive the story's drama. The same happens with heartbreak as your soul lingers in anguish.

As you continue to tell the dramatic story to others, or yourself, you BECOME that person again and then live out the same script with other people. You have dark clouds that follow you and can feel like the unluckiest person at times.

> *"You become what you think about most of the time."*
> – Earl Nightingale

Have you ever dated the same person that had a different face? You were sure that you left Tony and Tracey in the dust, but they keep popping up in your life, again and again, just in the form of Edward and Tiffany. You live the same script with a different cast, trapped in a negative cycle of your past.

Feeling like you can't escape the mental images and emotional turmoil in your body, you think you're depressed or anxious, but you are creating your own suffering by being trapped in the past.

When you share your issues with a therapist or psychiatrist, you tell the story from the lens of your trauma default. You have a spiritual and energy problem, but you are looking for a physical solution. There is nothing you can change outside of yourself that will free you from this cycle. It must be done from within.

No amount of prescribed medication, illicit drugs, alcohol, sex, or anything you do externally to soothe the pain of your ailing soul will relieve your pain. You must do the inner work to heal your soul.

Bless your past because it made you who you are today.

DEPRESSION IS DESTINY SUPPRESSION

"Trying to fix something, but you can't fix what you can't see. It's the soul that needs the surgery." – Beyonce

Depression is a state of mind, and it's my belief that being trapped in an unconscious mental state while replaying a cycle of trauma creates a pit that you fall in. Then, you remain there for extended periods because you are unaware that there is a different path to choose.

Depression is deep suffering and the body releases chemicals because it relives the trauma of the past over and over again. The resistance to letting go of an unhealed past or not choosing to do something different can result in deep depression to the point of immobilization.

This is a *decision*, but the decision is out of unawareness that you are the creator of your suffering. You are a victim of it, and you are continually being victimized by a story or a situation that occurred long ago that continues to materialize in your present reality. When you react in the present, your present trauma is a manifestation of the unhealed past.

Get busy doing this work so you can heal your past and then use that healing to go and heal others.

TOXIC RELATIONSHIPS

If you do not heal the past of a bad relationship and continuously think about that person and all the bad things they did, you will continue to attract the same person with a different face. By Law of Attraction, you become what you think about most of the time.

You create your present bad relationships by solely focusing on what you do not want and giving no consideration to what you do want. If you continue to focus on what to avoid, you will spare yourself from pain and trauma. But the very focus and thought of the past and what you do not want will continue to bring it into your existence.

Could this be why abused children end up in abusive relationships? Do they unconsciously seek what they try to avoid? Do they create them from the unhealed parts of themselves? Can you get the new love you want if you are holding on to all the tainted loves of your past? Or do you bring the tainted love of your parents who were tainted by the love of their parents into your relationship and wonder why they go bad?

It only takes one person to get healed in a family to break this pattern forever. Will you choose to do the work? Not for your glory, but the healing and saving of others, starting with yourself.

Unconscious actions and reacting from the mind of the wounded child will keep you in a perpetual state of suffering.

SELF-DISCOVERY IS A LONELY JOURNEY

Are you willing to be lonely and rejected for a season so you can reconnect with your Inner Being – Your God You? You will never be alone, and in time, you will be fully accepted by yourself and aligned with who you are meant to be in this lifetime, doing the work you were called to do.

The Law of Sacrifice is when you let go of something of a lower nature to receive something of a higher nature. Will you let go of your pain to receive healing? Let go of your anxiety and stress to receive peace.

Let go of your past relationships to receive the love of your life.

Let go of self-condemnation to receive self-revelation.

Let go of the unforgiveness of others to receive forgiveness of self.

Let go of the rejection of others and receive the acceptance of self.

Hurting people hurt people.

Most people are either going through something, going into something, or coming out of something.

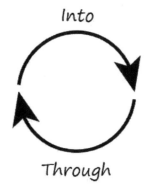

When you truly forgive yourself, you will be less judgmental and critical of others. You will have a greater capacity to extend grace because you know how easy it is to condemn yourself and how hard it is to forgive yourself. People are doing the best they can with what they know, and everyone is suffering with something from within.

PERPETUAL CYCLE OF GROWTH AND AWAKENING

For the awakened Being, you understand that you are not stuck in the exact same place. You are growing and expanding in awareness. You are rising in consciousness through negative experiences. However, because your trauma default is prevalent, you may feel like you're stuck or being pulled back with a bungee cord, but you are not.

As a spiritual Being, you are always in a perpetual cycle of growth and awakening, whether you're aware of it or not. Every new cycle creates the next level of awareness of self that needs to be explored and conquered. Like the children of Israel journeying through the desert for 40 years, the true journey should have only taken 11 days. They were in a cycle of growth and awareness and could not move to the next level until they learned the lesson at the level they were on.

Several times, they wanted to revert to being slaves. At least as slaves, they had a routine. They were fed, knew who they were, and what was expected of them, which was hard labor and being treated poorly. Playing small and being treated like they were small was familiar and expected.

In the wilderness, they were faced with discovering new things about themselves outside of bondage and the limiting expectations of others.

Sometimes they liked it, but most of the time, they didn't. Regardless of how many miracles were performed for them, they longed for certainty and security, even if that was in bondage.

When the children of Israel complained that they did not have any food and how they had pots of food to eat when they were slaves (trauma default), God provided them with manna and quail. God wanted to get them to see a greater version of themselves and to let them know they were free and had access to all they could imagine and more – The Promised Land.

Regardless of all the miracles they experienced, they grumbled and complained about the process and the journey. They never really saw it as an opportunity for self-discovery and healing. They didn't own the new mindset and blessings available to them, so they went in circles for 40 years and died in the desert, never making it into the Promised Land.

"Why are known hells preferable to strange heavens."
– Les Brown

They didn't get into the Promised Land because they were unwilling to release the limited vision they had of themselves and adopt the greater awareness of self available to them by God. They did not activate The Law of Sacrifice, letting go of something of a lower nature (limited perspective of self) to receive something of a higher nature (awareness of God-self).

However, the children born in the desert did not have the memory of "greater days in the comfortability of bondage" and moved ahead. When it was time for them to enter the Promised Land, they got access to a different food level, and the manna stopped.

As you continue your awakening journey and self-discovery, each level will unlock the next level of blessings for you. However, they can also be perceived as burdens because you can no longer do or consent to what you formerly consented to when you were unconscious and unaware.

What would have happened if they complained and rejected the better quality of food, having calibrated their taste buds to the manna? Would they have gotten to the next level? Probably not.

It only takes one person to get healed in a family to break this pattern forever.

BREAK THE CYCLE AND MOVE TO THE NEXT LEVEL

Many people are trapped in the cycle of going into and through something. Now that you are aware that life is a journey and you are expected to grow and expand, you will choose a different response to your trauma default and break the cycle that has been holding you back from being your greater self.

You will rise to the next level from the "coming out of something" cycle and bask in the glory of that achievement. But only for a season because self-discovery and healing different parts of yourself take a lifetime. When you break through to the next level, give gratitude for the place you have elevated to. Smell the fresh air, watch the flowers bloom, and feel the wind as it blows across your face.

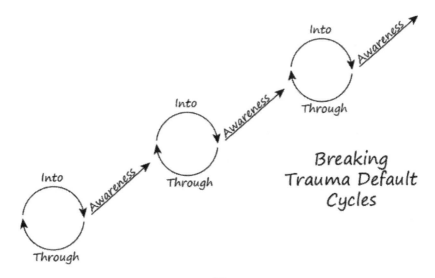

Take in the new level of awareness and all the things that you were once un-accessed at the lower level. They were available, but unaccessed. Inner peace, joy, wealth, prosperity, and health are always available to you. But because of the limited perspective of self you are living in at the moment, you don't seek access for what's already yours.

As you move into the evolution of your consciousness, the next level will be different. The ceiling will become the new floor, and you will feel a greater sense of self, but also a greater sense of overwhelm because you will discover just how great you are meant to be.

Take this next step in stride and understand that the Great Wall of China was not built in a day or even a year. It was a process that was created over time, brick by brick. The magnitude of your greatness and your responsibility to serve others, once realized, will completely overwhelm you. Don't shrink or fall back. Just live in the moment and build the Great You brick by brick, day by day, and as time passes, you'll marvel at how far you've come.

Awakened Beings understand that we are never done evolving and growing. We keep expanding, learning, and elevating our awareness, and serve until this physical body expires. Then, our spirit will reconnect with the Source and await the time we choose to return to another form to resume the journey, seeking new experiences and creating new awareness.

LET THE DEAD BURY THE DEAD

Don't allow the fear of your skeletons to keep you from seeking the inner treasure that will amass generational wealth for you and your family. The skeletons are dead and can no longer harm you. The problem is that every time you think about them or tell the story to yourself or someone else, you bring them back alive.

In fact, you are keeping these skeletons alive and fresh. Even if they are trying to die, you resurrect them back to life by telling the story of what someone did to you. Whether it's an old boss, your parents, or a bad relationship, you tell the story because you don't want to let them off the hook for what they did.

You are keeping your past and the skeletons fully clothed and nourished like the walking dead in your life, chasing and terrorizing you daily because you are unwilling to let the story go. Even zombies desire a proper burial and peace. Your unwillingness to let the dead bury the dead keeps them relevant and alive in your life.

You know the names of your skeletons. You know what they look like and what to expect. When you start thinking about them as you wake up and get ready for work, you get them ready too. You dress them up and spray on perfume or cologne. They walk out of the house with you, and you have a conversation or an argument with them during your commute to work.

They sit with you all day and flow through the bodies of the coworkers you despise the most. They go out to lunch with you and materialize in a rude customer service person. They become a conversation point with your friends during the ride back home or while you drink at the bar. They meet you in bed for a restless night and wake up with you the next morning to do it all over again.

You don't have peace, and they don't have peace. LET THEM GO. Forgive them, and they will no longer touch you or impact your life. You will break the energetic and spiritual connection to them, and they will no longer have access to your mind, body, soul, or dreams.

You are keeping the inharmonious and undesired spiritual connection that creates your agony by not forgiving them. Then, by the Law of Attraction, you attract similar people, scenarios, and experiences because that's your focus.

When are you going to forgive them and let them go? How many scenarios are you keeping alive with your thoughts and conversations? Is it any wonder that you do not have peace? Is it any wonder you cannot get a good night's sleep or seem to attract the mate you desire?

You are stuck in the middle of a nightmare all day and night, and you hold the very keys to your freedom - FORGIVENESS.

YOUR FREEDOM WILL CONVICT THE BONDAGE OF OTHERS

"Freedom is a messy and flamboyant process." – TD Jakes

When you seek freedom through forgiveness, you will stir up the negative emotions in others who have become comfortable being uncomfortable in a normalized dysfunction.

Some people love being miserable, and others don't know how they can be free. However, your desire to be free will convict them because then they'll realize that they too can be free but will choose to do what's easy and remain the same.

They will call you names and say you are selfish. They will say, "Who do you think you are?" Or that you think you are better than them. How does the decision for you to create a better life for yourself create such hatred and discontent in others? It's because they are unwilling to change and feel that if you change, you will leave them, and they will no longer have someone to comfort them in their misery and the unconscious behavior that is creating their suffering.

In an attempt to stay where they are comfortable complaining about their agony, they will try to sabotage you and your efforts to be free. Your friends and family will all join in to keep you where you are.

You may be in a ***good*** place - making good money, with a good job, and driving a good car, but your inner Being knows where the ***right*** place is for you.

You must be stronger than your desire to be comfortable and liked by your family and friends. You must be willing to separate relationships and sever ties with those who do not support you in your awakening. After reading this book, your primary goal is to increase your awareness so that you can reestablish the relationship with yourself.

The big You, your Inner Being – the Creator. It is lunacy for someone to tell you that you shouldn't want to reconnect with yourself to be happy and passionate about life. To live in the fullness of your purpose and be healthy mentally and physically so that they can be comfortable being around you.

When your growth convicts their bondage, they will try to shut you down and beg you to remain where you are, so they can have shared experiences and something to complain about daily.

Will you choose to remain the same, so you do not have to leave them? Break the shared dysfunctional habits you have chosen to call celebratory commonality. Your weekly wine nights or happy hours where you drown in the sorrows of the moment - which is your trauma default materializing in your present reality.

The lonely-hearts club, annual Valentine's Day dinner, or the singles cruise because you can't seem to find a mate regardless of how great you are. Surely there must be something wrong with eight billion people in the world that you can't seem to find and connect with the right one.

The moment you choose to stop singing the same old song and free yourself from the bondage of your past, you will open the door to a greater life. One that is filled with peace and joy. One of unconditional love, freedom, prosperity, and wealth in many ways.

Unconscious actions and reacting from the mind of the wounded child will keep you in a perpetual state of suffering.

FORGIVENESS IS A LONELY ROAD

The journey of awakening is being willing to cut negative and toxic relationships with others to be in a healthy relationship with yourself. It is being willing to stop wanting to be around people who allow you to be toxic, and you all thrive in your toxicity together and call that commonality.

Similar to the lepers that sat on the porches with other lepers. The unclean with the unclean and people with the issue of blood - all on one porch. You stay on the porch with them because you have something in common, and it is okay. They know you, your stories, and what makes you tick.

They say all the right words, hug you and ease your pain. They do not judge you or have any expectation that either of you can get better or should desire something greater.

All of that is okay until someone arrives and tells you that you can be healed. Many sick people remained on the porch, but few true believers chased the Messiah to seek healing. Jesus always said, "Your faith has made you whole." He never said He made them whole.

Each person had to demonstrate their belief in themselves before they were healed. When He told the man to stretch out his hand, the man had to believe that his hand would move first. When He told the paralyzed man to stand, he had to believe he could stand.

When He came upon the lame man by the pool, the man had to decide whether or not he believed in himself. I wonder about this man's commonality and telling the same old story of why he never made it into the pool. He was so comfortable telling that story that it became a part of who he was. A victim. A victim of circumstances. No one helped him. A victim of there were people faster than him—a victim of his own disbelief.

I'm sure in the early years, he believed in himself. But what happened? How many times did he try before he adopted the story? One, two, or five? Did he even try at all, or did he want to make the people around him think he was trying, so he had them walk him to the pool daily and bring him back home, never actually wanting to get healed but being needy and exhausting?

Pretending, but never really wanting it. What a burden to the people that dropped him off and picked him up. Or did they too have their own issues where they needed to be needed and felt obligated or joyful to take him to the pool every single day for years?

Did any of them challenge him to be greater, or did they just make the burden of carrying him daily a part of their stories of burdens of why they could not get ahead?

Surely, they do not have time to pursue their passion because they have to spend hours of their time on this task. Surely, they do not have time to take care of themselves because they have devoted their exhaustive energy to carry this man to and from the pool daily for years.

Is it that he depended on them for a healing he was never seeking or that they depended on him so they could use him as an excuse for why they never sought freedom on their own? Everyone was lockstep in their avoidance of the individual truth and the collective truth of their combined stories of interdependence to keep themselves on the bottom and never seeking anything greater. WHOA.

When Jesus prodded the man for answers, he spoke and had a cadence of his story and his carrier's stories that were woven into a tight-knit garment that he wore as a veil to cover his eyes from the Truth.

That he could (1) Free himself from himself. (2) Free himself from those who were comfortable with him in that state, and (3) Free others from their dependence on his story that is keeping them where they are.

He resisted, and Jesus asked, "Do you even want to be made whole?" That story had been told so many times that he stopped trying to do anything. Jesus said, "Pick up your bed and walk."

Jesus was just done with him and that story. Take your bed because you will never go back to that state again. Do not leave it there just in case you'll need it again. You will never need it again; you have been healed. Believe in yourself and your healing and throw that nasty bed away.

I wonder what happened when the man walked up to his carriers and showed them his healing. There may have been a few who celebrated.

Those are his friends in the new season of his life, and they will serve in a different capacity.

Then there were those who did not believe it and told him all the times that the very same miracle was temporary. They will dissect the story piece by piece and exploit the smallest detail to create unbelief. They will ask him if his legs are really strong or if he's tingling because tingling isn't completely healed. They will work to convince him that his healing is temporary to create unbelief, and within a week, they will be back to carry him to and from the pool.

They need to carry him to be able to say that he is the reason why they cannot get ahead. They will sabotage his healing for *their* story. Whether they consciously do it out of spite or unconsciously do it out of fear, the result is the same.

Then there are those who will outright reject the story and condemn him for being healed. They have attached their identity to his brokenness and will be mad that they are no longer his carriers.

Who are they now if they cannot carry him? Who are they now in their small belief that they cannot even believe in a miracle, even as the miracle stands up in front of them and professes it in their face? Wow! These are your greatest enemies, and you must separate yourself from people like this immediately and unapologetically, but not unkindly.

CHILD-LIKE FAITH

Matthew 18:3 – *"Truly I tell you, unless you change and become like little children, you will never enter the Kingdom of Heaven."*

Children are fearless. They will climb on a table and reach for something higher because, in their minds, there is nothing they cannot do. They have ingenuity and will create ways to escape their beds by climbing, extending, and reaching. Parents are shocked and appalled at the dangerous acts that kids engage in every single day. They spend their waking hours trying to convince their kids they are not invincible.

Kids take risks and do the daring. They will dress themselves in cowboy boots and tutus in the summertime. They will put on red polka dot shoes, yellow pants, and a blue shirt and swear that they are wearing the greatest outfit. They are immune to criticism and will wear their mismatched clothing proudly because they picked it out. Surprisingly, many adults will not criticize a child for their taste in clothing. They will celebrate them and encourage them in their desire to be independent.

If a baby doesn't start walking by 12 months, parents don't condemn them to a lifetime of crawling. They will cheer them on until they walk on their own. It is the nature of a baby to know that they are intended to grow and expand and have new experiences. When they try to learn how to crawl, they don't want to be held as much.

They want to get down on the floor and get busy moving in the direction that instinct tells them they are supposed to go. There is something within them that tells them that they should not settle for an existence of being a lap baby. They will try for months until they get it right. Once they start crawling, they will do it for a few months and then try to start walking.

A child's nature seeks to grow and expand and desires to experience new things. They are not afraid to fail or fall. They are not scared to try the same mundane task for hours on end, day after day, actions that many adults will become bored within a few minutes and quit.

What drives a child to want to do a mundane and repetitive task day after day? By instinct, they know that they are supposed to grow, lift their heads, roll over, sit up, crawl, and walk. To develop hand-eye coordination to pick things up and then feed themselves and eventually dress themselves.

CHILDREN ARE UNAPOLOGETIC

Discovering the Kingdom and becoming like a child is having the desire to be free and not caring how others feel about it. Hoarding your toys and not wanting to share; not speaking to people that you don't want to talk to, and refusing to smile at someone because your parents told you it's the nice thing to do.

You cannot make a toddler smile or speak if they don't want to. You can tell them to wave bye-bye 20 times, and they will not do it. Then after you give up and walk away, the toddler may turn around and wave. They do it at that moment because they want to and not when they are told to make someone else feel good. They do not shoulder the responsibility of doing or saying something to make others feel good. They will downright refuse, and parents are usually okay with that.

When did you stop being okay with other people not feeling good about you and making the decision to selfishly keep your peace and joy? To only wave or say something when you want to?

Believing like a child is believing that you will walk no matter how many times you fall. Believing you will run no matter how bad you are in the beginning or how many times you scrape your knees, fall on your face, or bump your head on the hard floor. Having the desire to explore the world and being curious and asking a million questions until you find the right answer.

Marveling at how ants walk with a big piece of food, and how bees fly with tiny wings. Why are some clouds fluffy and others are flat? Believing that you will wake up in the morning healthy and hungry. That you and your friend will make up quickly and be besties again, even though you shoved their head into a tree an hour earlier.

Believing that you deserve love from others. That you can be a fireman or a doctor or a singer, even if you are terrible at it. Kids believe anything and everything and do not limit their thinking to their environment. They dream big dreams and will profess them to the world or anyone who asks.

FIVE YEARS OF GROWTH

Think about how much growth a child experiences from birth to five years old. Have you changed that much in the past five years? Think about the growth between a 10-year-old and a 15-year-old while developing from a young adolescent to a teenager. Completely different things are going on in their bodies, height, and awareness.

Think about the massive growth from 13 to 18 as a young teenager develops into a young adult. Have you changed at all in the past five years? In the past 15 or 20? Pause and consider this question.

When did your inherent nature and instinct to grow and expand stop? When did you stop being curious about other things and people? At what point did you give up on life and settle for a meager and measly existence of sameness and a routine that you are bored out of your mind with?

Sleepwalking as you get ready for work. Driving unconsciously to and from work, not even understanding how you got there. Braindead at your desk while you hate your job and lament your coworkers. Sleepwalking through life.

The popularized show, the Walking Dead, depicts the daily existence of many people around the world. When did this become an acceptable existence *for you* and what are you going to do about it? Why did you stop growing?

Is it because of the fear of criticism? The fear of failure. The fear of people saying that you will look stupid. The fear of being criticized by your family and friends for stepping out and trying something different.

Has fear stunned your growth for the past 10 to 15 years and paralyzed you into a sleepwalking state of sameness and boredom? Has fear created so much pain in your body that you drink or self-medicate to soothe the pain of denying your inherent nature to expand and move forward?

You avoid, procrastinate, and distract yourself on social media, YouTube, or videogames for endless hours to ignore your stirring soul that is waiting to be awakened so you can grow and claim new territory.

CRITICISM DESTROYS YOUR SEED OF GREATNESS

What happens as life matures us? People stop complimenting and start criticizing. Over time, we condemn ourselves harshly before someone even utters a comment from their mouth. Women buy expensive clothes and dress up in the hopes of getting compliments but are greatly disappointed when they receive dirty looks and criticism.

As you grow up, people imprint their negative thinking and limiting beliefs on you. Your family will say, "We don't have the money."

"We can't afford it."

"No one in our family has ever done that."

"You will never amount to much."

"You're just like us, and you won't make it."

"You're too fat, too skinny, too black, too white, too tall, too short, too smart, too dumb."

Life will bury all that is good and cover the Light that you were born with. You develop layers of stories, lies, unbelief, negative experiences, and drama. But your Light never goes out. It's just been covered, and it is waiting for you to dig through the darkness, heal your wounds, forgive others, and rediscover your inner Being that is waiting for you to reconnect with it.

This is something you must do for yourself, although you do not have to be by yourself. You have to surround yourself with people who will allow you to separate from them for a season so you can heal. They will not be offended by your desire to be greater and try to sabotage you. They won't say that you think that you're better than them because you're finally taking the time to heal your wounds so you can take your place among the great spiritual Beings who are sharing their gifts with others.

But to get the Divine connections that will nurture you to your highest potential, you must let go of the people holding you hostage to a life you no longer desire. Those who tell you that you should settle for a good life when your God-self is calling you to a Divine life.

You do not energetically get what you want, you get what you have room for. You can't receive the new Divine connections until you let go of the old connections.

IT'S PRUNING SEASON FOR FRIENDS

John 15:2–*"He cuts off every branch in me that bears no fruit."*

When your friends no longer bear fruit in your life, i.e., nurture you, or encourage you to be better, be willing to cut them off. They are dead weight and are no longer useful in your life. They are a part of your history and not your destiny. Do not be confused. They are not **bad** people. They just are not the **right** people you need in your life to step into the fullness of your destiny.

Many people are unwilling to move forward into greatness because they do not want to leave their friends behind. They stay in misery for a lifetime and die in mediocrity, so they don't hurt someone else's feelings. They do not live like a child, but like an adult who would rather forfeit their future and sacrifice their family's generational wealth than to have the courage and dare to stand alone for a season. Be willing to be alone for a season to develop and nurture your seed of greatness within you.

William George Jordan said, "Man to be great, he must be self-reliant. The man who is self-reliant seeks ever to discover and conquer the weakness within him that keeps him from the attainment of what he holds dearest; he seeks within himself the power to battle against all outside influences… Be an oak, not a vine. Be ready to give support, but do not crave it; do not be dependent on it. To develop your true self-reliance, you must see from the very beginning that life is a battle you must fight for yourself."

Taking up the mantle to be greater will be the hardest decision you will make in your life. No one said that living in your Divine right would be easy, but people living it will tell you that it is worth it. Decide to step into your greatness.

FRIENDSHIPS CREATED AND NOURISHED IN PAIN

Eckhart Tolle talked about pain bodies in *A New Earth*. A pain-body is when you connect with someone based on shared common painful experiences of the past. If your dad walked out when you were a kid and met someone whose dad walked out too, you would energetically connect with them at that level of pain.

If your husband left you for another woman and you meet someone whose spouse did the same, you will connect with them at that point of pain. You will have more in common with them than someone who has been happily married for 20 years.

Their father walked out, and your father walked out. The shared stories of the pain and confusion of watching your mom struggle, being hungry, and not having good clothes. The shared pain of Father's Day, shame, anger, and resentment for not being visible for Daddy and Donuts.

Now you share the commonality of the pain of countless failed relationships and excruciating details of how each man or woman did you wrong.

Pain body connections include family members who have shared experiences of abuse, poverty, abandonment, or being disconnected from parents since they worked too much, or they went to boarding school, etc.

You spend countless hours in the comfort of complicit bondage, talking about a reality that no longer exists. You create pain for yourself day in and day out by continuing to resuscitate skeletons that are long gone but fully present and alive in your daily reality because you put them there.

You have a shared feeling of joy and a deeper connection because you found someone who truly understands what you've been through and what you're continuing to go through. The problem with connecting deeply from your pain body is that your good friend gives you permission to remain in that state by talking about the painful experience over and over again. They will strengthen the story of your pain and allow you to be justified in your anguish, further strengthening your story and your inability to choose to be free.

When you connect with someone's pain body, you can drag each other down into the throes of hell in less than five minutes. These conversations cloud your judgment and impact your awareness that you can be free from this deeply painful state. They will offer comforting thoughts because they understand your pain and will let you remain there for eternity.

When you want to be free and healed, you must become aware of who you're connecting with in pain and which pain-body they activate within you. Separate yourself from them at once.

BE RESPONSIBLE FOR THE ENERGY YOU PUT IN THE WORLD

Romans 12:2– *"And do not be conformed to this world, but be transformed by the renewing of your mind, that you may prove what is that good and acceptable and perfect will of God."*

When you decide to get healed, joy will feel foreign to you. If you have lived most of your life in self-condemnation, judgment, bondage, and pain, whenever you seek freedom, peace, and happiness, those will be foreign feelings to you. You have become comfortable with being uncomfortable in pain, so pain is comfortable, and peace will be uncomfortable.

Be aware and allow yourself to move through the new, weird feelings of having peace and joy and all the things you truly desire. Many of my clients panic when they have breakthroughs as they think happiness will be temporary and fleeting.

With this new awareness, the goal is to become an observer of how you show up in the world. Jill Bolte Taylor said, "Please be responsible for the energy you bring into this space." Getting healed and transforming through the renewing of your mind is not only about becoming aware of your circle, but it is more important to become aware of how YOU ARE showing up.

Consider the following questions:

1. How are you showing up?

2. What do you say about yourself to yourself?

3. What do you say about yourself to others?

4. What do you allow others to say to you?

5. What is the background story that plays in your head?

6. What scenarios trigger your trauma default?

7. Who are the people you attract into your life that have a shared commonality of pain?

8. Who are the people that you do not like, who are really a reflection of you?

9. Who soothes you in your pain and drama?

10. Who says negative things to you when you are having a great day and ensures you stay on the bottom with them?

Whew. What a list.

AVOID ENERGY VAMPIRES

Have you ever been around someone who was happy, and then they just turn negative and destroyed the whole mood at a social event? It's because joy creates pain for them. Whenever there is peace, happiness, and fun, people accustomed to drama and pain will create their own storms and then get upset when it rains.

They thrive in negativity and drama. They are pessimistic and chronically negative. Various social media channels are filled with these trolls who make nasty comments on people's posts. They come out of left field to do it. They also leave negative reviews on business sites, even if they have never patronized the business. They spread the filth of their negativity and spew it for others to experience.

When you engage them in a debate, you are engaging their inner chaos, and there is no way you can win that battle. Will you continue to surrender your peace to engage someone in a debate that is unhealed and full of pain?

Even if you feel justified because they said something offensive, the real question to ask yourself is, "What part of my unhealed trauma did they highlight for me?" Then get busy healing that part of yourself.

The same goes for relationships, friendships, and coworkers. There are plenty of lessons to explore. When someone says something to you that caused you to suffer deeply, was it really them, or did they trigger your unhealed trauma?

With this new awareness as you move through the journey of wholeness, you will use each offense as a lesson. You will see areas that need to be healed and not drown in pain or retaliate out of offense. Pain will be your greatest teacher.

DARE TO STAND ALONE

Let's be clear, if you want to be free, you will have to let a lot of people go. Some friends are here for a reason and others for a season. Even your long-term friends, if they are not on board for your healing, then they have to go too. Again, they are not *bad*. They just are not *right*.

Since family is forever, be willing to distance yourself from them for a season until you have clarity. Then, after you have healed, set healthy boundaries of what you will and will not tolerate. You may reconnect with most of your family, but some you will not.

You will have to retrain people on your new standards, and if they want to be in your life, they will adjust. However, if they are accustomed to you being dramatic, they will expect it and almost provoke you to see if you have really changed.

The most dramatic exits will be with the people whom you share a pain body with. As you seek healing and wholeness, they will not be able to find a connection with you anymore. It will disrupt their spirit, and they will try to bring you back to where you used to be so they can seek sameness and commonality.

You must be strong enough to detach yourself from these people so you do not fall back into that cycle of negativity. Dare to stand alone.

Dare to understand that life is a battle that you must fight for yourself. Dare to stand tall and strong like an oak and not reach to be connected with others like a vine. Dare to do the unthinkable so you can set your family free for generations.

GET A NEW CIRCLE

To keep you in bondage, old friends will bring up your mistakes and failures of the past. They want to put you in your place. They need to know how serious you are in your desire to be free. Hold your ground, and don't revert to your past. Seek new acquaintances and get around new people who don't know your past hurts, mistakes, and shame. They cannot show you a skeleton they don't know existed.

Healed people on the paths to their greater self will not tolerate someone who is trapped in their past and content with their misery. We are allergic to people like that. But we will also test your belief in yourself and will say, "Pick up your bed and walk."

It is up to you to make the first demonstration of your desire to be whole and healed; then, we will usher you along the way. If you reject it, we will simply walk away and leave you there and seek someone else who believes in themselves enough to want to be different.

THE IMPOSTER SYNDROME

The impostor syndrome is when you have a distorted view of yourself. Many highly successful people have two selves. Their work self and their home selves. Does this sound like you?

Your professional image is shiny and powerful. You are adorned with a multitude of degrees, awards, titles, and medals, and you stand 400 feet tall in your organization. You are an icon in your industry—a golden idol of yourself, standing tall for the whole world to see.

However, suppose you have not invested the same amount of time, money, and energy in strengthening your self-image and healing your trauma default. In that case, you will have a significant disconnect in how you see yourself.

The home you – the weak one that comes home defeated, burned out, and with a negative voice running rampant in your head. The one walking around with the skeletons of your past and complaining that everyone else is to blame for your inability to get to the next level. The unhealed child that's stuck in the trauma default loop.

The little you is three feet tall and no matter what you do, how many degrees you have, or how much money you make, you never really FEEL successful. The more you obtain, the greater the fear of being discovered is magnified, and the negative voice in your head gets louder. There is a struggle between ***who the world sees and who the voice in your head condemns.***

You aren't self-confident, and the higher you rise professionally, the bigger the gap becomes between your professional persona – your (golden idol) external projection of self – and your trauma default – your (unhealed child) internal perspective of self.

HIGH STRIKER

Comparing the gap between your professional persona and your trauma default to High Striker or the Strong Man Game – when you hit the scale with a mallet, based on how hard you hit it, the ball goes up. Your goal is to hit the scale as hard as possible to get the ball to strike the bell at the top, but eventually, the ball comes back down.

The gap between the 3-feet you and the 400-feet you is massive. You spend your days going up and down the scale, always striving to reach the top, and it is absolutely exhausting. The harder you work to hit the scale, the higher you go. The higher you go, the more celebrated you are.

People marvel at your external greatness, and you are rewarded for your achievements. You spend your days polishing your golden idol, and you may even spend days euphorically high if you had a big win, but eventually, you will have to confront the little you.

But the higher you go, the more fearful you become because you know it's a long way down. You also become angrier and resentful because that high feeling is euphoric but very temporary and fleeting. You can work yourself into oblivion, trying to prove your greatness by hitting the scale harder and harder, but you will always come back down until you strengthen your sense of self.

Many people work themselves into an early grave because they never realize they made it. They are fighting against the underlying story in their head of someone telling them they will never amount to much or they aren't good enough. They cannot even see their present reality of the big house, fancy car, material possessions, and a loving family. They spend their exhaustive energy and days at work to prove their worthiness.

But the voice they are hearing is from the past. Living from the mind of their past, they will drive their relationships into the ground, neglect their children, and spend their money on useless things that will never make them feel successful.

Does this sound like you?

PEOPLE SEE WHO YOU SEE

You spend your entire existence trying to fill in the gap with force and fighting. Then you wonder which level of you do people see. Do they see the 400-feet tall you or the 3-feet you? Which one are they judging? Are they judging you for being too big and thinking too highly of yourself? Or are they judging the small you and thinking you are nothing because you feel like nothing?

One of the best-kept secrets is this... *People see who you see.* Your greatest challenge to overcome is having an unpredictable and distorted vision of yourself. When you get angry at people for treating you like a nobody, could the cause be rooted in your subconscious belief that you are nobody?

Do you adjust where you are on the high striker scale to suit other people's preferences and expectations? The truth is you are both. You are the 400-feet tall person and the 3-feet person. The limited view from your childhood and your trauma default is the imposter. Not the great woman or man the world sees. Heal yourself of your trauma default and free yourself from yourself.

Do the work to discover your hidden and buried seed of Light and then invest time, money, and energy to personally develop the little you to merge the two you's. Then you will be unstoppable because you will know exactly who you are, why you are here, and what you're meant to accomplish in this lifetime.

With this life-changing clarity and awareness, you will not shrink from 400 feet to 200 feet to make somebody comfortable with you in your full power. ***When you are at peace in your power, they will be at peace with your power.*** You will not compromise your energy or your peace anymore.

TRAUMA DEFAULT BATTLES AT WORK

Are you trapped in a cycle of petty battles with your bosses and co-workers? Since the high striker gap gets larger as people ascend the ladder, the volatility of being exposed is unnerving. The executive conference room becomes the new playground.

Everyone's childhood trauma is battling for a seat at the table and triggering others. The worst disputes of people in team dynamics can be attributed to their trauma default and the particular coworker/boss who pushes that specific button. Some personalities will try to dominate the energy in the room because their father belittled them. Then, some will fold up and disappear because their mom was an alcoholic, and they had to stay out of her way.

When people can push your buttons and provoke a negative reaction out of you, they have found your trigger point that is connected to your trauma default. They can see the limited view you have of yourself and will exploit it to the smallest detail.

Many people who feel bullied by their boss or coworkers are reacting out of their trauma default. No one outside of yourself can create that much suffering for you. As you work on yourself, you will see that you are the cause of your anger, guilt, frustration, and shame at work.

These dynamics are on full display all day, every day in organizations around the world. It is time for you to become self-aware of how you're showing up so you can become an ***observer of the chaos and not a victim of it***. You will be able to play office politics better because you are not continually being triggered by the petty battles that happen daily.

BEING DEVALUED AT WORK

Not closing the gap between the two you's creates challenges in the jobs you apply for. If you feel like an imposter about your potential, demonstrated success, and educational achievements, you apply for small jobs. Then, you become frustrated when you are better than your boss and your boss's boss. This is a common challenge that many women have.

You tell your friends and family that your bosses are intimidated by you and then use that as a reason to drink wine nightly since you are being belittled and bullied. The truth is, they ARE intimidated by you because YOU ARE better than them.

However, you chose a small job, and you outshine them in every way. They do not like it, and it triggers the limited perspective of themselves and then activates their imposter syndrome and trauma default.

You are caught in a predictable cycle of trauma where your unhealed child is fighting their unhealed child. Then you report them to the teacher… ah-hem, I mean, HR for not treating you like you deserve. Heal yourself and break this cycle of madness. You will never win this battle and will end up mentally and physically broken because of this cycle's deteriorating effects.

WHEN THOU ART CONVERTED, STRENGTHEN THY BRETHREN.

Do not wait. This is the most important work you were called to do. Not your job, but your WORK to free yourself from your past so that you can go be a Light in someone else's pain. To free people from their self-made prison holes so they can go free others. This is the cycle of life.

When you are healed, people will see and believe you. You will have compassion and empathy for others in their deepest pain point because you've experienced that same pain and can not only extend grace, but you will demonstrate grace and *be grace* in physical form.

The people you are meant to serve will see you differently and be curious about who you are and what you do. You will become a physical expression of your spirit form. A physical vessel that the energy of God can flow through to serve others. This will not be done in a boisterous way like the people who practice religious dogma like the Pharisees.

You will exude grace for people in their brokenness and not judgment. You will offer comfort and not condemnation. You will know that everyone is doing the best they can with what they have and that most people are struggling with their own trauma default, so you won't hold them fully accountable for their actions – for they know not what they do.

When you speak, the people whom you are meant to serve will hear you and know your voice [His voice] because it will speak to the very essence of their unconscious and unhealed pain.

John 10:27-28 – *My sheep listen to my voice; I know them, and they follow me.*

LIFE IS SHORT AND UNPREDICTABLE

This lifetime is finite. It is short and unpredictable. To think that you have tomorrow to start getting on the path to your greater self is naïve. All you have is now. Start today to create a better tomorrow.

Your future is created with today's actions and thoughts and your willingness to forgive yourself and others for what happened yesterday. You can't change any of that. You needed all of it. Give yourself the gift of healing, and then you'll have the greater capacity to extend grace to those who need it.

Made in the USA
Columbia, SC
01 November 2020